A Dance With Me

Poetry & Prose

Sabrina Grancio

ISBN 10: 061557453X
ISBN-13: 978-0615574530

Cover art: Flamenco Dancer I by Caroline Gold

I. *Love*

II. *Loss*

III. *Life*

I.

Love

THE DANCE BEFORE THE DANCE

Meeting through a timid stare passed in a crowded room
I've been picked from all the other daisies
The way your eyes seemed to dance
Asking if I'd dance too
Hesitant to take a solid step
But anxious to get on with it
Searching for a speed to suit this demand
Want to reach out and touch your hand
Bonded to reality
Secluded by dreams
Reeling and sensing but feel a bit blind
Face to face with dawn and a sack full of time
The future holds all destiny
Awaiting my opportunity
Been weaving the master plan
Put a lock on this treasure with an irreplaceable key
Come, take my hand, dance with me

DAY DREAM

Let the sun shine down
Let the stars shine high
Let's walk barefoot through the clouds
Sit on the ocean's sand at night
Let there be music only we can hear
Let's conquer all we fear
Let's plant dream seeds
Feed them until they bloom for real
Let's double dare each other
Let spontaneous adventure take over
Let's picnic on a river rock
Bathe under a waterfall
Let's desert structure for a week or two
Entrust control to a full moon
Let's embrace our freedom
Sail on a boat named Genuine
Let's watch the sun rise
Climb the highest mountain we can find
Let's dance in the rain
Talk until there's no more words can say…

DON'T

Don't think you know
What I'm thinking
My thoughts go so deep
You'll end up sinking

Don't tell me
You love what you're seeing
When you haven't really
Seen me

Don't cry out
Your heart is bleeding
When it's wide open
Feeding the blood to me

Don't think you'll impress me
With your green-faced bills
Materialism is the only hole
Money can fill

Don't tell me
I'm wasting precious time
Within this hourglass
Are the sands of my life

Don't feel neglected
When I stare right through you
It's me I'm protecting
I don't play to lose

Don't expect to swim
Frantically in my blood
If you reach that stream
We'll be drowning in love

FOOL FOR TOMORROW

I'm a fool to think past tomorrow
But I'm well into the next day
Even if I am destined to wait
I've been staked
It's unlike me but somehow I could care less
A true nobleman came and I said yes
Still, there's something missing
And I know where it is
It is beyond what the mind says
It is a force that can't be escaped
Can't explain it even with paper and pen
Won't question it ever again
Somehow it's worth being held in that comfortable place
To kiss that beautiful face
To have that hand touch my hip
To let go of myself as is
This is my journey
It's my time to live
As selfish as it seems, I make this choice
As wrong as it may be, it feels too right to turn away
As much as he fights it, he thinks of us too
As removed as he is he knows his love is true

FANTASY OF DESTINY

A wild heart knows no rules
There's peace in the spirit world
The mind is a given tool
There's magic in the soul
The sun shone through the clouds
Like something was coming down
No miracle came really - -
Just a feeling of pure and the taste of honey
Facing the sunset, I see your shadow
Then turn to the dawn of moon
When the night mare comes for you
You draw like an archer would
Mark and hit
Luck pulls us in
I've searched long and you I come to find
All my senses are so alive
Opportunity knocks so I open up to get warm
Touch you so you'll know the chill is gone
You look at me with eyes of curiosity
And in a whisper I sing . . .
At the end of every mountain stream,
There is a waterfall
I'll be there if and when you call
At every closed door,
There is an open window
If you yearn for freedom
As so with the earth,
People do age
And so with the seasons,
People do change
The link is in me, is in you
I wonder, why be alone when it could feel this good?
I wonder about you

HOME

When life hits you heavy and hard
So hard that you just can't speak
When you're feeling weak in your knees
You can come to me
I'll hold your hand
I'll leave my light on
So you can find your way home

If you're blown over by the slightest breeze
When your gut is wrenching
And you just don't know which way to turn
You have a place to run
I'll renew your spirit
I'll leave my light on
So you can see that path home

If you find yourself in no-mans-land
When you feel like you're nowhere near anything
If you just can't take the world out there
You can come here
I'll warm your heart and soul
I'll leave my light on
So you can make it home

If your day seems like a nightmare
When you can't see clear
If you just can't choke back your tears
Never feel alone, my love
You can come to me
I'll hold you right on into tomorrow
I'll leave my light on
Come on home

LIGHT

The leaves all fallen
But my spirit is high
My friends all tried to keep me
But I'm running with desire
Don't know just where I'm going
Can't say I'll be back too soon
When the free wheel stops turning
Your light will guide me home

Dancing alone on the porch is no fun
I'll leave the back door open
You know you are the one
My friends tried to tell me
When you go, you're gone for good
It takes one to know one, I suppose
When the dense fog surrounds you
My light will guide you home

Instinct leads to what we know
Little did we know lust has its rules
There's no cage to tame our freedom
No question where and why
The clowns come and that circus goes
But even through the darkest hours
We're not out there on our own
The light shines on

MAN IN THE MOON

I see you
Through the deep dark indigo
I feel you
Pulling and powerful
So far out of reach
Yet so very close
I am so beautiful
Under you
Man in the moon
Release me from the inside out
Each time you boldly show
Take a piece of me with you
Until you captivate it all
Bare here with me a while
Man in the moon
Cast your beam upon my path
As I step into the mystery of tomorrow
Keep your force with me
No matter where I go
I woke this morning
Missing you
Come back for me
Shine bright for me
Man in the moon

PULL

The winter moon sits low
Rising slow but sure
A seductive eye watching me
And waiting with intriguing persuasive energy
I, too, am changing as I always knew I would
With each tender ray touching my skin
With each priceless face of a turning moon
I am willingly more and more exposed
Soothed by its passion and presence
Just what I've been missing most
A mere sliver slicing through this night - - just past new
I'm drawn to wanting more and more
I'm watching
And waiting
For the peaks of a full view

SHELTER

Spare a little shelter
Planning a fire
With your torch a blaze
Show me the way

Need a little shelter
Kindling a fire
Shed some light
Bring the sparks to life

With a little shelter
Building a fire
Give some heat
Throw me a flame

Under your shelter
Tending a fire
Passion ignites
Burning through the night

For sake of shelter
Feeding a fire
A fire we built
For you

STILL TIME

Whispers down long halls of task
Golden skin through open stairwell bars
Silent weeps of insecurity as I pass
Silent sensuous scenes
Desire runs free and fast
In the fresh rain
The freshness lasts
Enticed in to another's dream
Water beads down stone features
And down around the back
Ocular scopes slow and perverted
Unsuspecting prey
Familiar prey just the same
Beyond all hallway tasks
Peeking still through stairwell bars
Difficult to mask
Yet still masked
Afraid
Drink fresh rain
Dripping from the front on down
Enticed again
Desire runs free and fast
Cool beads of rain
Cool skin gold and hard
Gushing rivers over time
Time is still
Still translucent images
Frozen on one view
Still time

SUMMER DREAM

A man came to me one clear night in June
He arrived bearing gifts of glitter and pearl
Jewels not of gem but of eyes and teeth
He seemed to look right through me while seeing
every piece
His silent curiosity charmed me instantly
Thought to throw down my arms and forfeit the fight
But he was drawn to my strength, preferred my
head up high
He told his tale of toll and heartache
How he felt a void descending but then saw a light
He stood there before me cured and mesmerized
He journeyed long and far for this precious fleeting time
Believed a man untrue to himself is a man with no fire
True to this cause he revealed his warm weeping eyes
He whispered his intimacies, his fantasies,
his erotic desires
Vowed to protect me no matter what the demon's size
Proclaimed the love he had stored away was love to
last a lifetime
Held out a steady hand and beckoned me to his side
He led me to his sanctuary where through the night
we'd lie
Sipped exotic nectars so in our dreams we'd fly
There we drowned in the depth of each other's eyes
Touching our inner selves
Exposing our hidden truths
Bearing our naked souls
For me, he would wait the rest of his life
And for him, I'd wait the rest of mine

SUNSHINE AT NIGHT

The winter wind howls outside
It's cold here most all the time
It seems as if my time has come
And that this time is right
Something worthy has arrived
A fire's been started deep inside
I've seen the sun shine at night

We share ourselves by candlelight
We see the same, we think alike
From the serious
Through the silence
To the laughter
Never had a bad time
And the sun shines at night

He gives to me his wisdom
I return to him my truth
Another place to call my own
A place to let my guard down
I'm safe with him by my side
Because the sun shines at night

The smile he gives
When he touches my lips
The magic in his touch
When he caresses my skin
The way he whispers my name
When he holds me close
The look of relief in his eyes
When the sun shines at night

It's a bonus prize
A carnival ride
It's all natural
The best kind of high
It's comforting
It's peace of mind
It's the sunshine at night

UNARMED AND UNAFRAID

I've gone under and am in deep
To fall so quickly is unordinary
To care so fully is unlike me
There are many things I really want
But those things can wait
There are few things I really need
So, I ask you not to leave
They say one day love will find its way
You put my lone heart to rest and admit to loving me
The greatest fears that haunt me
You know I'll handle personally
Survival for me is a vital technique
A strength from you has reached me
And I've never felt quite so safe
At last it's alright to be unarmed and unafraid
It's you who gives
And you who receives
It's your hands that hold my hips
Your soft, full lips
It's you who's there through thick and thin
You who cares where I've been
It's your heartbeat that puts me to sleep
Your voice echoing through my dreams
It's you who's there when I wake
Your scent lingering

UNSPOKEN

Holding on to who I really am
Because it may just be all I ever have
There's no thrill in what life's been offering
Simply living year to year, day by day
To touch is not to feel, I say
To look is not to see
A little selfish, yes, I may be
Seeking someone with vision and feeling
I'm seen while not even looking
Says he saw me there waiting
It's been quite a journey since someone's
got the best of me
But here and now, it's happening
Enjoy me
Join me
Don't speak, release me instinctually
Give and take everything
Laugh with me in the rain
Tease me
Please me
Don't speak, just hold me
In our kingdom of ecstasy
I'll be queen and you'll be king
Among the dragonflies and the fairies
Bathing in rivers of tranquility
There we'll live in perfect harmony
Here we are, what do you say?
Yesterday took with it those empty years
Today tells the tale of what will and won't be
It all depends on what we really want from here
Don't speak, go on and show me

WAIT

Each day our eyes don't meet
My heart breaks
Each day without our stroll
My spirit sinks
Each day our hands don't touch
My fingers ache
Each day without your voice
I choke back the pain
Each day without your energy
Is a day I don't want to be
Each day I wake up and hope
But you are not there to greet me
Each day I wonder
Each day I wait

II.

Loss

ALFIE

The last mile
Their last smile
The end of the party
The end was that Friday
Does the cost of life
Compare to a bottle of beer?
Is the exhilarating speed
Worth a mother's tears
Reality of tragedy strikes so strong
For all those undeserving and so young
Time will carry on
As will fond memories of those we've lost
Will death this close to home teach us to know
When enough is enough?
Will we be able to save the surviving ones
we love so much?

COLD SEPTEMBER, WARM DECEMBER

Weeks into winter
But it's been like New England Spring
Mother Nature surely felt the rumble of the
Towers coming down
One, then again
A senseless awakening –
"Why?!" we all cry out in pain
We join our hands around the world and pray

She's holding off December's freeze
For our reconciliation and cleansing
Mercifully the earth there is still soft enough
For those Union boys to do their gut wrenching job
Sifting through the rubble; memorizing every remain

A bounty battle will come to pass
We're sure to win, but it won't bring them back
We'll erect new statues
With new found virtues
Finding our own truths in between

Don't take this life for granted, a lesson truly learned
This morning's sky whirls and swirls
The colors are quite spectacular
Timeless energies in celestial flight
Together, as one love, from the other side

GRAY EYES

Gray eyes
Poised and profound
Hints of penetrating purple
Gray eyes
Empty eyes
Stormy
Tired
Gray eyes
Looking at me
Seeing me
Mahogany
Gray eyes
Tones of deep blue
Dancing to jazzy blues tunes
Celebrating
Gray eyes
Following me
Watching me
Pondering
Gray eyes
Reflecting cool autumn skies
Lingering
Comforting
Gray eyes
Touching me
Feeling me
Belief in me

In memory of my grandfather, John A. Capone, Sr.

MOVING ON

Where we going
Where we from
Where we going
Moving on
Summer breezes through the door
Strips me of my senses
Turn to find you there
Bring it on, bring it on
Waiting on that rain to fall
Cleanse us of our faults
Fear no more of each other, of ourselves
You said yourself you'd be a fool to go
Waiting on those leaves to fall
Turn to find you gone
Suspended
You had to go, I know, I know
Waiting on that snow to fall
Whiten out this dreary town
Hoping you'll call
You can't pick up that phone, I know
Won't show yourself, I know, I know
Waiting on that fresh spring dew
Looking for you
Miss you in this room
You're too far gone, I know
Where we going
Where we from
Still holding on for you
You keep moving on, I know
Don't waste my tears on you, I know, I know
Won't wait for you anymore

THE PILL

I call your number
Then hang up the phone
Don't know why I'm calling
You don't hear my words

Look for your car
Down at the boat launch
Don't know why I stop
You wouldn't notice me while I watch

Listen for your voice on my phone mail
Don't know why, it's late
You're tucked away in dreamland
You're lying next to someone else

I pace the floor like a wild animal
Feel trapped in this pre-programmed world
Don't know why our paths had to cross
The night is black, not even a moon to curse

Drive the back roads to work
Sing every word to those love songs
Don't know why I kid myself
Remember you said, there is no hope

I'm not your girl
That's the pill I ate
You weren't meant for me
Too many years too late

QUITTER

Close my eyes to try to forget you
Keep my mind occupied doing stupid chores
I want to hear you don't *want* me
Tell me you don't *feel* me
I want to turn and run, escape for good
Beat myself up cause I can't figure it out
My gut says hold on
My head says no
What the fuck?
Don't want to hear your voice
Just want to turn it off
Don't want to play this game, I give up
Tried to get on your agenda but it's all about you
And here I go again pouring out a fool
Don't want to be a whim anymore
Or a pawn in your power struggle
Too few and too far is how it adds up
Never got time for anything else
I'm more than that
I'm sure of that
You'll never know how much
I'll never win your respect
Never had it right up front
Don't want to hear your bull
Or even the lies I tell myself
You've been self-serving
But I need some giving
I've been crusading
But you never asked for my help

RAVENOUS

The blue sky fell black
A raven's curse
You wear the claws and dig, dig until it hurts
You blew in with the wind
Kindled a fire, watched it burn
Then blew out with the smoke again
I'd never seen a more selfish look
I lost a friend, you know
The flame came from your eyes
And I was blind because I didn't see inside
I didn't then but now I do
I can see the real you
The rain hasn't called me since then
There are still ashes smoldering
Your act of innocence won't work on me
Little miss carefree
There are things to care about
Things worthy of respect that you choose to neglect
Ignorant to the cost or loss
You're quick to stick your hand in someone else' pocket
Trust in you is a blown circuit
You seem to see people as your puppets
Jealous of everything you can't call your own
You make an art out of freeload
A gambler's game
A sprinkle of gold but filled with dust
Living on an edge that's sinking quick
A bag of used up old tricks
For a long time I kept faith in the blood line
But it's been lost somewhere between the stories and lies
I was the fool to hold my hopes up so high
They burnt down with the blink of your eye
I'm through with giving you make up time
I'm picking up the pieces and taking what's mine
I'm moving on to excel in life
I'll start here by leaving you behind

REVENGE

Perverted illusion
Full of empty words
You've got your quick wit and charm
To get what you're after
'Cause you just can't bear to be alone

A double edged sword
Jab it in through flesh and bone
Twist it all around
Slip it out fresh with blood
Then it's back to square one

Suck 'em in, spit 'em out
To you that's what it's all about
You strut down the glory line
From the posh to your old local haunts
Just to say you've had 'em all

It's just too easy to tell the truth
Weave and bob till you can find a way out
Break out your little black book
Make them all jump through hoops
'Cause you know for you they would

You stood there laughing when I was down
Hey you, with all your teeth falling out
Yeah you, behind those big iron bars
Who's laughing now?

SUNSET

I have a secret; kept it long and well. Life is short; what
can you do… some things you just can't control. The
flood gates opened and the walls came down. Time
stood still. Tried to run, but it was too powerful. I gave
and he took. I waited for those precious minutes - -
and I understood. He said he couldn't live without it and
I believed every word. He said I was beautiful. He said,
"I . . .

I tried to please all his senses -- to touch him from the
inside out. I tried to show him what I knew the first time
he saw me and I turned and smiled. I tried to keep him
close -- tried so hard it hurt. So, I mark this page and
close this book. He's going, all knowing and my journey
goes on now too.

He's trapped, stuck, no way out. He never knew me; I
never had a chance in hell. When he was good and ready,
not one bit more. When his ego was in crisis he'd give me
a call. When my heart was breaking I wrote these words.
My heart was breaking with the sun going down.

He smirks like a king but squirms like a boy. He
whispered my name - - his own tear fell. He choked his
heart back down his throat and said, "…but I belong to
something else." Remember my taste in your mouth.
Remember that number on the door. Remember me;
I'm the one who freed your soul… Remember, I . . .

Don't forget this sunset
Took me high and left while the sun set
Bit a big juicy peach chasing his sunset
It was all just a dream and the sun set

The sun set

III.

Life

AMONG THE SHADOWS

She dances in the darkness of her room
She dances to forgive all those
She fights the light even when it feels warm
She dances in the darkness all her own

She dances in her way, in her form
She dances and she mourns
The spirits lift her and move her on
To mend her torn world

She is a lily
She is a birch
She is a sculpted stone
She wears the feathers of a warrior

She dances in the darkness of her room
Turns to the door only to turn back around
She cries out then bites her tongue
She dances in the silence all her own

BARFLY

Don't go too far
Don't swim to deep
Don't dare life to kiss you goodnight
You might just get what you ask for
Don't blindfold emotion
Damn it, look at me!
Facing up has got you on the run
Facing up has got you drowning
Keep drinking down that stupid juice
Keep snorting up those big fat lies
Get off that stool, barfly
Where you going to go when the check runs out?
Going downtown and setting your price?
Who's going to give you a free ride?
You're out of the loop; you're losing your mind
Get off that stool, barfly
Your face is pitted deep with lines
You have become what you've always defied
Pick yourself up and take back your life
Get off that stool, barfly
You're running from losing but we all lose sometime
Talk to me, let's go for a ride
This bar room is eating you alive
Look around, my friend, open your eyes
Get off that stool, barfly

THE CITY, USA

Yellow lights leading me into the city
Everyone on the street is in such a big hurry
We're chasing the big carrot, making holes in the cheese
A rat race we justify as modern-day society
Everybody has to have their stock in the game
Everybody's looking for their claim to fame
Women chasing their careers down the drain 'cause their
Baby-sitter was late
Hoping instead of a pink slip, her companionship will get her
a break
She forgot to pick her son up from little league
Husbands putting their wives to shame 'cause his new assistant
is real tight and sweet
Hasn't seen his family in weeks, but they own a second home
in the country
He forgot to show up at the little league game
Do we make time or is enough time just a pipe dream?
Not looking anyone in the eye on the train 'cause it makes
you a target for crime
If you don't learn to hustle, this city will eat you alive
Talk today is too damn cheap; remember when your word was
all you had to give?
Now all you need is a plastic card with a line of credit
Do you help the old man or let him fall in the street?
Is he working his con or could he be a genuine human being?
Does that young punk hail Hitler or just shave his head?
Does he even know what that swastika means?
Digging your own ditch of debt to keep up with fitting in
Year after year, trend after trend
Simplicity vanishes as the essence
Too much is never enough takes its place
There's always going to be a corrupt cop on the beat
Working the circle of drugs instead of keeping our kids
off the streets
Hard to believe all the politicians aren't completely full of shit
And based on their slick looks and charm,
We're the ones voting them in-
What's going to happen when technology crashes?
What's going to lead the way?
We'll really have to see each other eye-to-eye, face-to-face
I think long and hard and yes, for the children, I am afraid
The sunrise leads me out of the city
Damn, the clear blue sky looks pretty

CONTEMPLATION

Maple fire
Birch bark on the lawn
Tip toe on the rooftop
Look out down below
Faint voices pushing me closer
Don't want to hear it any more
Maybe this time I'll fly
Maybe this time I won't
There may be no sense in me or in these words
Not much makes sense any more
Nice to know a friend thinks to call
It cradled the fall
Just restless ghosts making noise
Eager loves come and gone
Most don't offer up much
But take what they want and keep on going
Days long over and much better off
Never saw life as clear as right here, right now
Knowing exactly what I want
From exactly where I stand
Yes, well, I haven't been far
But it's been a long road
Let the sky burn and the ground fall
Hell, I made it this far
Fresh, clean, focused straight on
It's all music now
So, red robin whistle me a prayer
Hey, blue bird, keep me company awhile
Here among the weeping willows
Follow your heart
Trust your gut
These are the days I'm living
With this new music from now on

FEBRUARY

Quiet is the night
The stars sunk deep into the sky
The clouds much more revealing
Quiet is the night
Delicate New England trees
So bare without their leaves
Quiet is the night
A simple powder of snow
Protected by a shield of ice
Quiet is the night
Icicles on the lights
A pool of water frozen in time
Quiet is the night
The grass like a sheet of diamonds
Sparkling in the moonlight
Quiet is the night
Sleek winter apparel
Glowing fireplace
Quiet is the night

FLH

The sound of rolling thunder
The ground trembling under my feet
The smooth running motor
The scent of worn leather
An American tradition
Uninhibited freedoms
Not just a want, more like a need
The never ending passion to ride
A true and unrelenting high
The intensity of our connection when we're in each other's
presence
The excitement that runs through me when I feel the
vibration
First and third, baby, first and third
Off just cruising
Destination unknown
Slip it in higher, baby, we're really moving now
We could head west toward the pacific coast line
Or to a northern mountain side
Maybe we'll just chase the moon
Only stopping long enough to quench our thirst and refuel
The perma-smirk on your face
'Cause you'd much rather be no other place
My thighs pulled snug around your waist
You and me on your FLH
Listen to those pipes rip through the night
As we claim our space on the smooth strip of highway
Feel the crisp air through your hair and on your face
Breathe in deep, revive your life
All the brothers and all the sisters alike
Ride to live, live to ride

THE GRIST MILL AT NOON

The water falls and the big wheel spins
Here at the old grist mill
I'm back where I've been many times before
This sturdy old oak still here for support
As I sit alone and have a talk with myself
Where I've been, where I want to be
The sun is stifling hot, but still, I face it
The dream that seems so distant, but still, I chase it
The little house made of stone walls;
Yet inside, the nourishment it produces
Like these walls I've built around my heart
With the love to give, but who will ever feel it?
The trouble is, who to trust and when –
Who do I dare to let in?
The deception I've known and the pain sacrificed
The bridges I've crossed that nearly killed me,
but I survived
The strength I'll need not to give in to defeat
The drive I'll need for all the odds there are to beat
The question is, have I still got it in me?
The best I can do is trust my gut instincts
Jaded by emotional warfare, it won't be easy
The scent of lilacs and the sound of children's laughter
Is incentive and a sweet reminder
To retreat would only rob me of what I'm really after
I'll keep searching for that love I need
I know it's out there

HUNGER

She stares north down the railroad tracks
Then back at the tracks she's made
As sure as hot steal sticks to those rails
She's off on another run without a plan
Daddy's out of sight and mother doesn't care
She's free to go just about anywhere
She follows those tracks to a northern beach
Wakes with a head full of sand and hunger pain
Got to get to a southbound train because
her addictions plead
She likes the little blue beans and the white ones,
so pretty
Whiskey, neatly, to numb all her pain
The laughing and laughing and laughing
Slowly going insane

LIVE NOW NOT LATER

We're all at the mercy of our mother nature
She'll nurture us along as long as we let her
She'll keep sharing her brilliant colors as long as we protect her
In testing conditions, do you gear toward stronger or weaker?
Only a fool would underestimate her power
In moments our lives could wash away -
Be ready

We're all a mixture of what our lives had to offer
We're all bound by one vice or another
Just one more drink or that last secret lover
In the office working on the thirteenth hour
A passive-aggressive compulsive shopper
Take a good look around –
Its happening

We all seem to be hoping for a forgiving savior
Would you be a firm believer is those doubts weren't in
your way?
Would you have made it this far without your
grandmother's prayer?
Would you succumb to death peacefully or would you
fight it all the way?
When the time comes, we are simply plucked away
There's no time to waste –
Have faith

Could it be that one lies to protect one's self or simply to
deceive another?
Would you rather know the truth no matter how much it may
hurt you?
Is it safer in the shallow end because the risk of depth is just
too much to handle?
Do you hide under the hair color and make up because you're
much too vain to go natural?
Is that your genuine opinion or something you bought in to?
Does exposing the real you make you entirely too vulnerable?
It's not too difficult to see right through you -
Have courage

ME, MYSELF AND I

I am a woman with pride
Nothing or no one will push me aside
I am a delicate touch, yet strong and tough
Nothing or no one to rob me of what I've earned so far
I am who I am through and through
Nothing or no one to strip me of that truth
Through this life I move on
And through it I become
Entertained the highest highs
And wept of the lowest lows
Through the darkness I see light
Past the death I find life
I am a woman who fights for her cause
Nothing or no one could make me stop
I am open to opportunity and endeavors
Nothing or no one to stand in my way, not ever
I am receptive to new ideas and suggestions
Nothing or no one to make my final decisions
With this passing time I grow
From a tiny bud
To a full grown flower
With that little bit of sun
And that little bit of shower
I bloom into my own absolute power
I am a woman who knows what she needs and wants
Nothing or no one will knock me down
I am a woman who knows where she's been and
where she's going
Nothing or no one to keep me from growing
I am a woman with heart and passion
Nothing or no one else can make it all happen

NANTUCKET

An invitation of smile to inner working worlds
Brass locks with silver keys
Try, try the test and see
We follow right along
Guided by what we believe
We follow the promise
We believe
Secrets kept at sea
Dreams become realities
Tick, tock, chime
Nothing is for free
Some are strong, some are weak
Peaks and valleys maze
One way or the other
On a quest for peace
Get but give more
Give it up but be sure
Now is no matter for what's in store later
Churn, churn, till we're sore
Wish full bottles wash ashore
Ocean lover's ashes galore
Nature takes her course

OBJECTIVE PERSPECTIVE

We, the drivers
The survivors
Remote control bombs
The filthy rich with their marble floors
And decorator lawns
The dirt poor, they're hungry
And chained down
Livestock feed on the lucky farms
Good bye to the grave old
Good luck to the new born
Life in perspective
Adapting to every change
In search of a place to call home
Snow caps and cacti
The ocean from a whale's eye
Might keepers of an oil mine
Majestic birds with the power to fly
True natives of the sky
The silent tiger, cunning and wild
Fights to keep its hide
Ignorance from one who roams free
Though the power of money and technology
Care is owed to this earth
Care is owed by all of us
For the apple trees and the sunflower seeds
For the air we breathe and the fresh water springs
Yet, there's wildlife on the brink of extinct
The seas are weak
The sun's burning out
And the soil's too weak to heal itself
We in all our glory
We in all our greed
We in all our narcissistic craze
Will surely kill ourselves
We'll surely find a way

SEASONED

I may keep my key way down deep. I may have been beat down, torn up, cast away, stripped and blamed. But I salvaged a little something from a whole lot of nothing. I may be weathered and tired but I walk tall and'll look you straight in the eye. I may not have been to every place but I've been far within myself. I know who I am.

I may not make six figures a year. I may not live in a million dollar home. I may not belong to a posh country club. I'd trade all those extra rooms you never use for soft sand, a campfire or a cool waterfall. Hell, my favorite jeans cost twenty bucks but I know who I am.

I may not have a manicure. I don't obsess over my weight. I may be a dime-a-dozen brunette - - nothing too spectacular among fluorescent lights and stark walls but I can transform into something that will knock your eyes out. A passionate, perceptive, all-natural girl, yup, that's me and I know who I am.

I don't conform to all the rules or commercial ideas. I don't need a reason to drink good champagne. I'm comfy in silence, in work boots and leather clothes. I ride my Harley until the day is long and I've partied with the best of the misfit toys but, brother, I know who I am.

I don't kiss ass and I know when I'm being fed a good line of shit. I'm not afraid to laugh out loud and if the tears are there I let them fall. All the asshole snobs in the world can think I'm not good enough. To hell with their superficial games! I know who I am.

I am an unmistakable energy that most will never know up close. I am a free young spirit no one will ever control. I understand my needs and wants and my motivations for both. I don't wear fancy lace panties every day but damn straight I know what turns me on. Yes, oh yeah baby, I know who I am.

A ship came to shore to explore my world. I am the light that guided the way. Through the sweet spring scents, the summer heat, the bold colored leaves and the winter freeze, it silently swayed. I am the mellow breeze. That valiant ship dropped anchor here in my bay; I am one good reason to stay.

SIX O'CLOCK NEWS

Where's the sanity
As I open the refrigerator door
There's something missing
It sure as hell isn't in there

What's the use in sweat and tears
No sense in bringing another life here
The gap is cold and widening
The local news is just plain scary

The crazy, spinning, train-wreck feeling
The end is gaining speed
Pen to paper is null and void
Nothing left to say; no one left to hear

Can't understand it
No rest for the weary
Won't ever understand it
So much wasted but not enough to eat

See the child, her eyes are swollen
Hear her cry, she cries herself to sleep
See the children who've been beaten
Then watch the children self-destruct

Victims lose their entirety
Justice is a twisted nightmare
The system is weak and rotten
Belligerence is everywhere

TAXED

Homeless with no shoes
Royals with piles of gold
Frustrations of a labor man
He's got dreams and goals
And a fear he'll never win
Dictation from a big boss man
He's got a swivel leather chair
And wears a greedy grin
Innocent children
Born into a world of political bullshit
Only to grow
Into a tax bracket

THANK YOU

It's not because of you
As a result of you
Or for you
But I owe my thanks to you
For showing up
For the chance to be bold
For the movement forward
Intentions or no
Thank you
For the drive
For proving that elusive chemistry does rise and shine
For being true to you
And inspiring me to be true to me too
Thanks for asking the questions
For having a talk
For saying I'm pretty when I feel like I'm not
For having integrity and being honest
Thanks for sharing
Beyond the typical
Aside the practical
That it's not just a myth
Romantics do exist
For helping me know there is so much more
In me
Out there
Thank you

VERMONT

The moon still kept its mystery
Far away from any city harm
This morning's fog held a security
Here in mystical Vermont
So refined way up here on the mountain
Like the calm after a storm
The candles we designed add richness to the charm
And the gypsy woman who read our dye-stained palms
The intrigue of what's beyond that stream we found
Is enough to make our imaginations run wild
A graceful doe keeps close to her two fawn
And we keep close to our site fire's warmth
In awe of the show of lights the stars put on
In the midst of these spring water pockets
And distant cry of wolves
The miles of antique stone walls and broken fences
Scattered relics of lives in these fields that once flourished
But now all the crops are gone
I guess sometimes one just has to pick up and move on
Trying not to leave regrets behind
A mix of sweet green scents and sharp mountain lines
This peace I feel inside
Dirt roads and river rock farms
Harmony with no sound guiding us along
Knowing right now I belong right here in Vermont

ABOUT THE AUTHOR

Sabrina Grancio was born in Boston, MA

in February of 1971.

She earned her BS degree, graduating Cum Laude, from

Northeastern University in Boston, MA.

Sabrina currently resides in Massachusetts.

A Dance With Me is her 1st debut as a published author.